T0010996

PEP TALK

THE WORDS AND WISDOM OF THE CATALAN MASTER

A GILEZINHO BOOK

First published 2022 by
Elliott and Thompson Limited
2 John Street
London WC1N 2ES
www.eandtbooks.com

ISBN: 978-1-78396-672-1

9 8 7 6 5 4 3 2 1

A catalogue record for this book is available from the British Library.

Illustrations by Isobel Mehta

Printed in the UK by TJ Books Limited

'Children very young, they must play, just play. Play and play and play and play, just play.'

PEP GUARDIOLA

'Pep's work goes beyond something tangible. The legacy he leaves in his teams is much more about the "how" than the "what". That is why he is so special. Pep's ability is to transmit, to convince others, and to reach the mind of the footballer. The way he communicates drags everyone towards his way of playing. The most complicated thing for a coach is not preparing the strategy – it's touching heartstrings. He is a master at that.'

MARCELLO LIPPI

PEP ON . . .

FOOTBALL

'**Football is emotions.** It's tactics,
definitely, but it's also emotions.
Without the ball, we are a team with
desire and passion to regain the ball
from the first minute to the 90th.'

'There is one rule in football when you
have the ball and that's not to lose it.'

'**Luck doesn't exist in football.**'

'Football is the simplest game
in the world. The feet just
have to obey the head.'

'Each night when you are going to
sleep, ask yourself if you like football
or not; ask if right then, you'd get up,
grab the ball and play for a bit. If the
answer is no, that is the day to start
looking for something else to do.'

2. PEP ON . . .

MANAGERS

'When I was fourteen, I said I'd be a manager and win thirty titles. I'm so pleased to have been a part of incredible groups of people at Barça, Bayern and City. I'll always be grateful. They are incredible numbers in a short time. I have a feeling that every time it gets more difficult. Achieving is so nice, so good.'

'People always think the coach is the strongest person at a club, the boss, but in truth, he's the weakest link. We're there, vulnerable, undermined by those who don't play, by the media, by the fans. They all have the same objective: to undermine the manager.'

'Before every match I lock myself up in an office with pen and paper and watch two or three videos. I take lots of notes. That's when **that flash of inspiration comes** – the moment that makes sense of my profession. The instant I know, for sure, that I've got it. I know how to win the match.'

'The manager who wins is a genius and the manager who loses is a disaster. People still don't understand that it doesn't work that way. Sometimes you don't win because the margins in that competition are so tight. If Sergio Ramos kicks the ball and they score the second goal, the City manager would have been a disaster and decisions from Zidane were perfect. That is why you must be calm and know exactly what happens in the games. We know it as a team.'

ON HIS MENTOR

'This was how Johan Cruyff worked. He was demanding a lot, but when you got there, and you were in his team, **he was an incredible protector**. He would push and push you, and then he would protect you. He was a master at handling players.'

'We all feel that hunger in football. With Cruyff, it was different. He deepened and changed the hunger, so you became conscious of why you are getting better.'

'Cruyff is the trainer who made me suffer most. With just a look he gave you **shivers that could chill the blood**.'

'Sooner or later I will be a coach. I'll train any level offered to me. Someone just has to open the door and give me a chance. I've no pretensions that I'm ready to work at a higher level yet. This is a process, a learning curve. The first steps are vital and **there are no second chances**.'

'I think when you are training at 72, it must be boring at home. Our job is nice. You are working with young people, athletes, in competition. Every game is different. Maybe that's why Roy [Hodgson] and the other older managers do it. I am not going to retire next week or next year, but I don't think I will still be a manager at that age.'

'There are talks that just come to you and talks that begin from a few ideas based on what you have seen. What you can't do is study the talks, learn them by heart. Two or three concepts are all you need, and then you have to put your heart into it.'

ON JOSÉ MOURINHO
'José is the dog's bollocks in front of the press. I can't compete with him there. But I would remind him we were together for four years. I know him and he knows me . . .'

'We're similar in the sense that we both want to win, but apart from that . . . Our paths are very different.'

'I know Mourinho only too well and he's trying to provoke me into a reaction, but it won't work. I'm not going to react. **Only when the time is right**.'

'We will play a football game. Sometimes I win, sometimes I lose. Normally he wins, as his CV shows. We are happy with our smaller victories, which seem to have inspired admiration around the world.'

'As Mr Mourinho has called me Pep, I will call him José. I don't know which one is Mr José's camera. They must be all of these. **In this room he is the f**king boss, the f**king chief**. He knows the ways of the world better than anyone else. I don't want to compete with him in this arena, not even a second.'

AFTER MOURINHO RECOMMENDED PEP SHOULD GET A FIFTY-YEAR CONTRACT AT BARCELONA

'Fifty years! Look how much hair I've lost after just two!'

'With Mourinho, so many things have happened. So many things . . .'

'Ego is the source of the majority of a team's problems.'

AHEAD OF HIS HUNDREDTH BUNDESLIGA MATCH
'I haven't lost a lot here, I am sorry. But considering how little I lost, I have got a lot of stick. Not only me – others got it too, from Allegri to Conte, Capello, Sacchi, every one of them. Today in our profession, nobody gets any respect.'

ON MIKEL ARTETA

'He is above, above, beyond a good manager. The character, the personality, leading…he is incredibly loved by all of us.'

'Often when I don't know something, I act in front of the players as if I do. I do it so they believe I have the answers and that gives them the confidence to play. Sometimes they ask you about things in life, and then you must adopt the role of a father, brother and son.'

'I wonder why we do press conferences if you don't believe what coaches say?'

'You have no idea what it means
as a player when you are losing, or
things are going wrong, and a
coach tells you the reason.'

'When I'm not energetic and feel a
little bit drained or tired, I'm pretty sure
I will quit. But right now, I feel good.'

'When you're in charge of something,
you always have to bear in mind that you
can leave. I work better thinking that I
am **free to decide my own future**.'

ON DIEGO SIMEONE

'There is a misconception about the way he plays. He is more offensive than people believe. He doesn't want to take the risk in the build-up, but after that, they have quality. I'm not going to talk one second about these stupid debates.'

'I admire the ability to resist, resist. They know at some point the bee will sting.'

ON JÜRGEN KLOPP

'He is the biggest rival I have ever had in my career. Jürgen makes world football a better place to live. He's a good guy and I don't have any problems with him. If we win, I'll invite him in. And he's said many times that we are a rich club, so the wine will be perfect – high quality.'

'As Jürgen has said many times before, titles are just numbers. **It's the emotion that people feel** during the ninety minutes that they're watching us that is the real reason we're in the job.'

'The day I see the light go out of players'
eyes, I'll know it's time to go.'

'I am a better coach now than I was,
and in ten years' time I will be better
than I am now.'

'I'm so happy here. I'm not staying
forever but I would stay forever. There
cannot be a better place to be.'

3. PEP ON . . .

ENGLAND

'As a player I was unable to realise my dream of playing here. This league is something unique – the feelings of the fans, the media and the players' style. I hope in the future to have the opportunity to be a manager here . . .'

'In Barcelona, Bayern Munich; in Spain and Germany; we were able to do it. But people say: "You only did it because you were in Barcelona and Bayern Munich. You will not be able to do it in England!" **So, let's do it . . .'**

'Going to England is a risk, but
that is why I like it.'

**ON WINNING HIS FIRST TROPHY FOR MANCHESTER
CITY, AGAINST ARSENAL IN THE 2018 LEAGUE CUP**

'The first half was not good – too many
mistakes with simple passes – but the
second half we played with more courage,
more personality. That is why we were
outstanding after the break. This win is
not for me, it's for Manchester City.'

**THEN THE PREMIER LEAGUE, WITH A
RECORD-BREAKING 100 POINTS**

'We cannot deny that this season we were
good. Every single day. The big clubs in
England, they have a lot of trophies and a
lot of history behind them, so sometimes
you have to do these kind of things to make
you believe: "Wow, we are good too."'

**(DESPITE LOSING 3-2 AT HOME TO
MANCHESTER UNITED)**

'I don't understand. We are the team
with the least goals conceded.'

ON RETAINING THE TITLE IN THE TREBLE-WINNING 2018/19 SEASON

'I have to say congratulations to Liverpool of course. They helped to push us and to increase our standards from last season. It's incredible: 198 points in two seasons. Normally if you get 100 points, the tendency is to go down, but Liverpool helped us to be consistent. To win the title we had to win fourteen games in a row. This was the toughest title in all my career, by far.'

**REMINDING JOURNALISTS CITY WERE NOT THE FIRST
TREBLE-WINNERS (AFTER ARSENAL LADIES)**
'The first time men's. The women,
they won it.'

ON A THIRD CONSECUTIVE LEAGUE CUP IN 2020
'Three times in a row is a big success.
It's the consistency and being there
every day. It's incredible.'

ON FIXTURE CONGESTION

'Of course it is too much to expect. All the managers complained about it, but they don't care. A distance of two or three days again and again. The players suffer. They want to do well and the clubs have a lot of pressure to win or qualify for the Champions League. **We push and push. The body says "stop", "enough".** With that number of games, the players break down. I can be tired – and I don't run. For them they'd enjoy it more, the people too. People can live without football for a while. It's too much. They can go to the theatre, to the cinema, restaurants, to watch the fireworks.'

'The doctors say that you need four days to recover eighty per cent of the effort you have played before. Imagine doing that in two days, and after that three days, and after four days. That is too much. But they are not going to change. I know that.'

'Are you saying that we're the smartest? That Omicron doesn't come to visit us? We had a lot of cases and injuries. We played Aston Villa with eleven first-team players. The last six, seven games, there are four, five academy players on the bench. We are in the same situation as all other clubs. It's around the world. The virus comes to the bubble, everyone suffers.'